A STEP BY STEP BOOK ABOUT
OUR FIRST AQUARIUM

ANMARIE BARRIE

Photography: Dr. Herbert R. Axelrod; Dr. Sylvan Cohen; Dr. Stanislav Frank; Michael Gilroy; Shuichi Iwai (Midori Shobo); T. Kumagi; H. Kyselov; Dr. Kenneth Simpson; Dr. D. Terver (Nancy Aquarium, France); Lily Pons Garden; Hans-Joachim Richter; C. E. Smith; Edward C. Taylor; Ruda Zukal. Humorous illustrations by Andrew Prendimano.

Distributed in the UNITED STATES by T.F.H. Publications, Inc., 211 West Sylvania Avenue, Neptune City, NJ 07753; in CANADA to the Pet Trade by H & L Pet Supplies Inc., 27 Kingston Crescent, Kitchener, Ontario N2B 2T6; Rolf C. Hagen Ltd., 3225 Sartelon Street, Montreal 382 Quebec; in CANADA to the Book Trade by Macmillan of Canada (A Division of Canada Publishing Corporation), 164 Commander Boulevard, Agincourt, Ontario M1S 3C7; in ENGLAND by T.F.H. Publications Limited, 4 Kier Park, Ascot, Berkshire SL5 7DS; in AUSTRALIA AND THE SOUTH PACIFIC by T.F.H. (Australia) Pty. Ltd., Box 149, Brookvale 2100 N.S.W., Australia; in NEW ZEALAND by Ross Haines & Son, Ltd., 18 Monmouth Street, Grey Lynn, Auckland 2 New Zealand; in SINGAPORE AND MALAYSIA by MPH Distributors (S) Pte., Ltd., 601 Sims Drive, #03/07/21, Singapore 1438; in the PHILIPPINES by Bio-Research, 5 Lippay Street, San Lorenzo Village, Makati Rizal; in SOUTH AFRICA by Multipet Pty. Ltd., 30 Turners Avenue, Durban 4001. Published by T.F.H. Publications Inc. Manufactured in the United States of America by T.F.H. Publications, Inc.

Contents

Fishkeeping as a hobby has become increasingly popular during the past few years; it is now among the world's most popular hobbies, ranking near photography and stamp collecting. This phenomenal growth of interest is attributable to a number of factors.

INTRODUCTION

Scientific and practical knowledge in this field has expanded to such an extent that it is now possible to reproduce most aquatic environments at home. Aquarists today derive an enormous amount of pleasure from their hobby, whether they maintain a simple aquarium in their living room or an ornamental pond, complete with fish and plants, in an outdoor garden. The life cycle of fishes, plants, and other aquatic forms is easily observable under almost ideal conditions in a home aquarium. Just watching fishes swim in an aquarium is relaxing, entertaining, and surprisingly educational; and breeding aquarium fishes can be interesting and very profitable.

Properly displayed, an attractive aquarium is quite a conversation piece. It is not only ornamental, but soothing to the spirit as well as entertaining. Doctors recommend it to relieve tension.

A terrific experience for children, an aquarium allows them to care for dependent creatures and to learn about biological life cycles in the process. Fortunately, the tank is simple to maintain; the fishes are easy to care for, and they never need to be "let out." These aspects also make an aquarium suitable for shut-ins.

Compared to other domestic pets fishes are extremely

FACING PAGE:
Angelfish *(Pterophyllum scalare)* live long under the
proper conditions. They are best purchased as
juveniles, not as adults which are relatively
expensive. Many varieties are available, including
albinos and solid black.

quiet so there's no need to worry about disturbing the neighbors. In addition, acquiring the fishes and setting up the tank can be relatively inexpensive and the subsequent costs minimal. All sizes and shapes are usually available at nearby aquarium stores.

Should you decide to travel for a few days, your fishes will survive rather well without your having to ask someone to care for them daily. Fishes can live for several days without food.

A Little Fish Biology

Most people are familiar with all the typical fish characteristics: a streamlined body, fins, gills, large eyes and mouth, and scales.

Many fishes have a streamlined shape that conforms to the laws governing the displacement of liquids. Their bodies exhibit the least resistance when moved through water at the speeds at which fishes swim.

The three main functions of the fins are stabilization, braking, and locomotion. Muscular contractions of the tail and body actually provide the main propulsive power. The dorsal fin(s) along the back and the ventral fins on the belly stabilize the body to prevent it from rolling. The pectoral and ventral

A fancy goldfish called a lionhead, a variety with no dorsal fin. Developed artificially by man, it is not found in the wild.

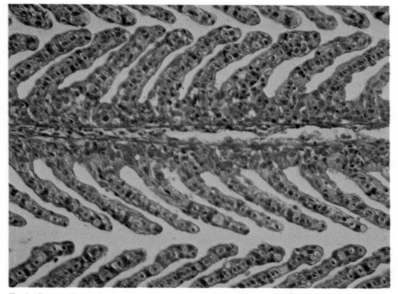

Each finger-like process in this magnified gill filament is called a gill lamella. This is where the exchange of respiratory gases between the water and the blood takes place.

fins balance, brake, turn, and offer some propulsion. The caudal, or tail, fin also lends to turning, stabilizing, and propulsion.

Oxygen is not available to most fishes unless it is dissolved in the water. Therefore, fishes draw water in through the mouth and filter it through gill membranes to obtain their needed supply of oxygen. The oxygen is absorbed into the bloodstream and the water, together with carbon dioxide and waste products, is discharged. The absence of lungs and the presence of gills are among the main features separating fishes from higher vertebrates.

The nostrils of fishes are connected to neither the respiratory nor alimentary systems. They are merely simple pits containing scent buds, yet their ability to detect blood and other odors in water is well established.

Fishes have an internal mechanism capable of picking up vibrations from the water. No external ears are present, be-

cause the ears of fishes lie entirely within the skull.

Most fishes have adequate eyesight for a given range. The eyes are usually large, lidless, and barely moveable.

The bodies of most fishes are covered with overlapping scales. These hard plates are set beneath a thin layer of epidermal tissue for streamlining and protection against injury and infection. The size of the scales varies with the size of the fish; as the fish grows, so grow the scales. Barring accidental loss, the specific number of scales remains constant throughout life. A fish's age can be determined, sometimes, by the growth rings on the scales.

Products that allow aquarists to regulate the relative acidity and alkalinity of the aquarium water are available at pet shops and tropical fish specialty stores. Photo courtesy of Fritz Pet Products.

Water

Some ordinary tap water may be put directly into the tank without further treatment. More often, though, the condition of the water is unsuitable due to the presence of chlorine and an excess of dissolved gases. "Conditioning" the water is a strongly recommended safeguard.

Water is conditioned, or aged, simply by having it stand for a week or two in the tank before introducing any fishes. The conditioning process facilitates an exchange of gas between the water and air, permits fine organic particles to set-

Aquarium reflectors come in two basic styles: full hoods, which cover the entire top of the tank, and strip reflectors, which cover only part of the tank. They also are available in two different bulb types, incandescent and fluorescent.

tle out, allows fish parasites to die before finding a host, and gives time for bacteria in the water to strike a "balance." Your local petshop will have chemicals to remove chlorine and chloramine from the water.

Do not be alarmed should the water become cloudy after a few days. This is a completely natural phenomenon attributable to an increased bacterial count and will clear itself within a week. Your aquarium shop might have nitrogen-fixing bacterial cultures with which you can inoculate the tank and achieve a "balanced aquarium" sooner.

Light

Light, be it natural or artificial, is mandatory for successful maintenance of an aquarium. About 12 hours of light per day is optimum. Fishes need light to see, feed, and reproduce. Light also has a definite effect on the fishes' color. Dull illumination is sufficient for most fishes but more adequate lighting is a necessity for plants. Artificial light may supplement natural light or be used as the sole light source. The control of plant growth and the suppression of plankton and algae are easier with artificial light only.

Artificial light must be bright and close overhead. It typically takes the form of a low power bulb or strip light, about 2½ watts of standard illumination per gallon of water, fixed into the aquarium lid. The overhead light is usually enclosed in a reflector to increase the light thrown into the tank.

Care must be taken to avoid overheating. Fluorescent lighting is preferred because it emits less heat than standard bulbs. Another advantage with fluorescent light is the reduction of glare. Use only those fluorescent bulbs which copy natural daylight most closely or are specifically designed to give light best suited to plants and to bring out the color of the fishes. Petshops sell special fluorescent tubes designed for the aquarium.

Fluorescent lights are more expensive to install but cheaper to run than standard bulbs because they throw out more light per watt. This translates to a reduction to energy costs; because of this, it is highly recommended that you use a fluorescent tube.

Temperature

The best temperature for individual freshwater aquarium fishes varies among species, but a temperature range between 74 and 78° (23-26°C) seems suitable to most. Waters of higher temperatures have an increased bacterial count and a reduction of dissolved oxygen. Sudden temperature changes tend to cause shock in fishes, followed by disease.

Aquarium heaters should have an outside adjustment for controlling temperature and a well-built contrivance for fastening the heater to the side of the aquarium. Multiply by 5 the gallons of water the aquarium contains to calculate the correct wattage. Since heaters are not available in 5 watt multiples, get the closest you can.

Every tank needs a thermometer. Many thermometers are fixed or float inside the tank. Newer strip thermometers adhere to the outside of the tank and change colors to denote temperature changes.

Introduction

Digital thermometers are very easy to install, cost very little and under the proper lighting are easy to read.

Location

The aquarium should be located in a position to take advantage of any available daylight, but not direct sunlight. Near a window is preferable, but the tank should not be in a position where the sun shines directly into it and overheats the water. Elevated temperatures kill both fishes and plants.

Avoid locations near heaters and radiators that can warm the tank and cause overheating. Air conditioner vents and other drafty spots must be shunned as well as rooms, such as kitchens, that experience abrupt fluctuations in temperature.

TANK
SELECTION

There is a limit to the number of fishes an aquarium can adequately maintain. This restraint is influenced by the size, species, and condition of the fishes to be kept as well as the temperature and aeration of the water. Exchange of gases between the air and water is the most important factor in determining fish capacity. This is why the surface area of the water, not the actual volume of the tank, concerns us most. The surface area is found by multiplying the length of the tank by its width.

Assuming a temperature of 24°C (75°F) and no mechanical aeration, 1 in. of fish (excluding the tail) should be allowed for every 24 sq. in. of area. In a case of a 36″ x 12″ x 12″ tank, the surface area would be 432 sq. in., which divided by 24 yields 18. This is the number of inches of fish that can be put into the tank. More fishes might be placed in the tank and not seem distressed, but they won't flourish as well. As the fishes grow they must be thinned out to maintain the original 18 inches.

These numbers are only approximations to be used as guidelines. Adjustments can be made for circumstances, such as increased aeration, relevant to individual tanks. Do not use the numbers of fishes a petshop keeps in its display tanks as a guide. The fishes only stay there a week or so and are constantly being thinned out. The situation is not comparable to the home aquarium where the fishes are long-term residents.

The size and shape of the tank are crucial because there is a definite limit to the number of fishes an aquarium can successfully accommodate. You should know the approximate number of fishes you plan to keep in order to select a suitable tank and equipment; or, alternatively, determine the space

FACING PAGE;
A tank can be a part of the decor of a room. It can
serve as a focal point of admiration and
entertainment for all, adults as well as children.

In determining the number of fish that an oddly shaped tank can accommodate, one must take into consideration not just the total volume of the tank but also the surface area.

available and obtain the largest size tank that will fit into that space.

The most important consideration when selecting a tank is the ratio of the surface area of the water exposed to air to the volume of the water. For example, two containers could hold the same volume of water but the surface area could vary considerably. A shallow aquarium offers the greatest surface for a given volume. Therefore, theoretically, the aquarium should be as shallow as possible to maintain a good replacement of oxygen to the water. However, extremely shallow tanks are unsightly, so a compromise is usually made between biological and esthetic requirements. A general rule is to have the tank wider than it is deep. Most tanks are at least twice as long as they are high.

Tanks are available in a wide assortment of shapes and sizes. Bear in mind that smaller tanks cannot accommodate a decorative selection of plants and fishes, a numerous amount of fishes, nor any large fish. Large tanks, though, involve greater expense but less difficulty in servicing.

To compute the capacity of the tank in liters, multiply the length, width, and height in cm. and divide by 1000.

$$\text{liters} = \frac{L \times W \times H}{1000}$$

To work out the volume in cubic feet, multiply the length, width, and height in inches and divide by 1728.

$$\text{cubic ft.} = \frac{L \times W \times H}{1728}$$

Fresh water weighs 8⅓ pounds per gallon or a kilogram per liter. The depth of the tank determines the amount of pressue exerted by the water on the glass. Too often tanks are made with secondhand glass or glass that is not of an adequate thickness. See that your tank is of unblemished, new glass of a heavy gauge.

Keeping fish in a small confined area is not recommended. Even when provided with some aeration to supply oxygen, the accumulated metabolic waste products will kill even the healthiest and hardiest fish.

Mostly glass tanks are sealed with a silicone waterproof compound and are therefore unlikely to leak. Regardless, check for a faulty tank before setting up the aquarium! Place the tank on a flat, solid surface and fill it with water. Leave it for several hours and then check for pools of water on the table top. If a leak occurs it may be repaired by using one of the many strong, modern adhesives available. If the tank is new, contact your dealer about replacement procedures.

All tanks need to be fitted with a water-resistant

cover. A tank cover prevents fishes from jumping out and other creatures from getting in, keeps the water warmer, and slows evaporation. Most tank covers sold in petshops will have been prenotched. Notches of suitable size are cut to accommodate heaters, tubes, and such other accessories. A small feeding door eliminates the need to remove the entire cover.

Vibrator air pumps are available in many different sizes, so they can be tailored to the size of the aquarium and the number of pieces of equipment that they'll provide air for. Photo courtesy Rolf C. Hagen Corp.

Weight is the most important consideration when choosing a stand. Commercial stands are available for all standard tank sizes. The majority are painted angle iron and have a lower shelf for storage. Attention must be given to warping if the aquarium is placed on a wooden stand.

Aeration

Surface movement and circulation of water within a tank are vital. In fact, the best way to increase fish capacity is water movement, usually supplied by aeration. The fish population can be as much as doubled with an aerated tank.

An aerator aids in the circulation of water, which exposes a greater surface area of water to the atmosphere. This facilitates the absorption of oxygen and more importantly serves to remove excess carbon dioxide and other harmful gases from the water. It is actually the amount of dissolved carbon dioxide, not oxygen, in the water that is the limiting factor

in determining fish capacity. The objective is to have as low a carbon dioxide content as possible. Reduction of stratification (cooler water below, warmer above) is another advantage of aeration.

An aerator is an apparatus that introduces a regular supply of air into the tank of water. The usual method is to force air through a porous "stone" situated at the bottom of the tank. The air emerges as continuous streams of tiny air bubbles.

An aerator is reasonably silent and the electrical consumption is quite small. Thus it costs relatively little to run. Your petshop will probably have a large variety of air pumps to show you.

Filtration

A filter should be added to help keep the aquarium crystal-clear. Contaminants are filtered out as water is shifted from the tank into the filter container, passes through layers of porous material, and out again into the tank.

Filtration is also aeration because the water is constantly flowing into and out of the tank. It may be quite unnecessary to install additional aeration equipment in a suitably filtered tank. There are many types of filters. Some are placed under the gravel; some hang outside the tank; some cannister types sit on the floor; etc.

Consult with your aquarium shop or read a larger aquarium book (like Dr. Axelrod's *Exotic Tropical Fishes*) to learn all the facts.

Power filters actually are small water pumps; they are very efficient at both filtering the tank and providing good water movement and aeration. Photo courtesy of Rolf C. Hagen Corp.

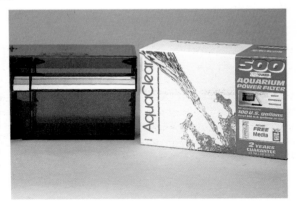

The aquarium must be furnished to make it look attractive and to provide the fishes with more natural living conditions. The layout is determined by your imagination, so show off your artistic talent!

FURNISHING THE TANK

Gravel and Rocks

The purpose of aquarium gravel is to provide decoration and to hold down rooted plants. Sand packs too tightly to permit penetration of the roots and the finer gravels provide more surface area for bacterial growth. Plants will get little grip if the gravel is too coarse and uneaten food will lodge between the stones and putrify in the water. The best bottom covering is fairly coarse gravel with a variable grain size.

Rinse out the dust and dirt even if the gravel was purchased as "washed." The gravel may then be placed in the tank and sloped upward from the front of the tank to the back. The slope best exhibits the contents and allows debris to collect toward the front of the tank where it can be easily removed.

Placement of rocks and wood in the tank provides cover for the fishes and renders a more natural looking environment. Their surfaces must be reasonably smooth to prevent the harboring of uneaten food particles. Extra care should be taken in the selection of rocks as those with a soluble mineral content may be toxic to the tank inhabitants. Hard, insoluble rocks offered for sale in petshops should be sterilized by boiling before use.

The location and arrangement of the wood and rocks are a personal matter, but a natural looking landscape, complete with hills and valleys, is desirable. Correct usage of the proper materials makes it possible. Ornaments such as divers

FACING PAGE:
A person who is handy may be inclined to build his own aquarium stand, but for most aquarists it is best to buy the stand at your pet shop.

Echinodorus cordifolius is one of the many popular varieties of swordplants available for the aquarium.

and treasure chests are popular for children's and ornamental aquaria.

The best time to introduce the water is after landscaping. Slowly add the water so as not to stir up the bottom. Gently pouring the water onto a saucer placed on the gravel helps to minimize disturbance.

Plants

A large number of varieties of water plants are available. Plants often contribute more to the attractiveness of the tank than do the fishes. Some aquarists cultivate plants for their own delightful visual effect and not just as decorative adjuncts in an aquatic display.

Cryptocoryne lingua is from the Far East originally, but like many cryptocorynes it is raised commercially for hobbyists who want live plants in their tanks.

Aquarium planter strips and pads can be used to anchor live aquarium plants beneath the gravel bed without interfering with root development. They also help to hold nutrients drawn from the water in the aquarium at the roots of the plants, thereby fertilizing them. Photo courtesy of Aquarium Pharmaceuticals, Inc.

Plants have several functions in a tank: as hiding places for timid fishes; as a spawning medium for many types of egg layers; and as the vegetable matter that most aquarium fishes require in their diet. A complementary biological exchange exists between fishes and plants as well. The plants use fish waste as fertilizer.

There is no reason why an aquarium should be without plants. Both live and plastic plants can be purchased from most tropical fish shops at a moderate price. Live cuttings are not an absolute necessity. In fact, plastic plants may be a better choice for beginners. The artificial growths won't die while the novice devotes his attention to the fishes, but aquatic gardening is fascinating.

Before installing the plants they should be thoroughly washed under cool running tap water to remove any insects. Ideally, plants should be quarantined before introducing them into a tank. Certainly do not collect your own specimens from rivers and ponds as they may harbor parasites and disease germs. If possible, only buy plants which are already rooted in small pots. Plants with naked roots are much more difficult to propagate.

A gravel depth of 8 cm. (3 in.) at the back and sides of the tank provides for the higher and larger growing plants to be sited. Smaller plants are positioned more to the center, and a plant-free swimming space in center front lets the fishes display themselves well. An engaging setting is acquired by trial and error, and it may be necessary to move the plants several times to achieve the desired effect. Make a plan before you decorate your aquarium.

The best method of planting bunch plant cuttings is to bind three or four sprigs together with lead (not copper) wire. Cut back the roots of rooted plants to a length of 3 to 5 cm., according to the size of the plants, and then anchor them into the gravel using a forked stick. Be careful not to bind the stems of bunch plants too tightly or the wire will act as a tourniquet and prevent rooting. Leave small spaces between rooted plants to allow for subsequent growth. After two or three weeks the cuttings should have rooted and new green shoots will appear. Potted plants are merely stuck into the gravel—pot and all!

The plants must be kept wet because even a short period of drying may kill or damage them severely. A convenient planting technique is to fill the tank half full with water. When the planting is complete, the tank can be filled the rest of the way.

Some aquarium plants are quite colorful, like this *Hemigraphis colorata*. Note the reddish undersides of the dark green leaves.

The plant with deeply incised leaves in the foreground is *Hygrophila difformis*, popularly called water wisteria.

All green plants require sufficient light for photosynthesis, and water plants are no exception. The tank should be placed in a fairly bright location but never in such a position that the sun can shine into it. This will cause overheating and may kill both plants and fishes. Artificial light should supplement the daylight to keep the plants flourishing.

When the tank is finally set up and planted, it is advisable to wait at least one week before introducing any fishes. The water needs to "mature." Live plants will act as a conditioner and tester of the environment. If the water is too "raw" as to be unfit for plant life, then it is unsuitable for fishes as well.

Maintaining the Tank

Obviously, when considerable time and effort have been put into making an aquarium as attractive and natural as possible it is important that this be maintained. A well-balanced tank should not require a great deal of time for upkeep, perhaps only thirty minutes a week.

Fishes become acclimated to a particular environment and do not take well to sudden change. In fact, it is possible to "over-maintain" a tank; fishes and plants will suffer if they are

Only those fish species with similar requirements should be considered for use in a community tank. Temperament is of great importance. Never include larger and aggressive species.

Furnishing the Tank

Except during breeding, angelfishes are peaceful to each other. In order to protect their delicate fins from damage, keep biters and nippers out of their tank.

disturbed too often. It is best, therefore, to change the aquarium on a gradual, routine basis to clean out pollutants not removed by a filter.

Every week replace 15-25% of the tank water with fresh aged (or treated) water. A replacement of aged tap water is suitable as the chlorine and excess dissolved gases will have dispersed within 24 hours. After the water is drawn simply condition the water a day or two in an open container; aerating it will help greatly. Introduce this water gradually into the tank to avoid a rapid change in temperature.

Automatic aquarium water changers available on the market are a suitable alternative to the manual replacement of water. Test kits for pH, nitrates, hardness, and ammonia content are also useful commercial aids. They give the aquarist helpful information to maintain proper water conditions.

After a few weeks the aquarium will become "mature." The correct oxygen:carbon dioxide exchange has become established and algae may begin to appear. Most species of algae are beneficial in limited quantities as they provide

Netting a live fish requires patience and the right technique. Observe the salesperson in the pet shop you patronize and study the method employed closely. He or she may also give you some helpful hints in netting different kinds of fish if you ask.

some fresh food for the fishes. The main problem with algae is their growth on the inner glass surface of the aquarium makes it difficult to observe the contents. The inside of the glass should periodically be scraped with a razor blade or a special scraper designed for this purpose. The surface can then be gently wiped with a sponge until it is clear.

Inspect the tank for any dead or dying leaves and shoots. These can be pinched off with the thumb and forefinger and discarded. Prune those plants which have grown too large. These cuttings may be retained for planting in another tank or planted in another section of the same tank.

Netting

Never actually handle small fishes and certainly do not handle fishes any more than need be. It is rather difficult to catch a fish with the use of a single net without inflicting some slight injury. Minor abrasions can be the site of infections which may spread throughout the entire tank. A fish can be safely moved, but once a fish has been established in a tank for a long time don't move it unnecessarily. Fishes become adjusted to a particular environment, and on occasion transfer to a seemingly suitable tank is fatal.

Nets for catching fishes should be as large as possible but not very deep. They should curve gently, without points, to minimize the risk of injury to the fishes. Fabrics with a wide mesh offer less resistance to the water. Synthetics are popular because they dry with a shake and are not quickly rotted. Nets with plastic-coated frames discourage rotting at the edges of the netting material. Two nets make fish catching much easier.

Try to slip the net under the fish and lift it out cleanly without creating havoc. If your patience fails before you secure the fish, stop and try again later. If you decide to chase the fish more aggressively success is unlikely.

Shown is a net designed for pond use. The frame is strong and the handle thick and long. The net is flat at the bottom; wire supports provide a platform where the fish rests as it is lifted out of the water.

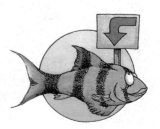

SELECTING FISH

Letting the tank mature for several weeks ensures that there are no leaks, the plants are settled in, the temperature control functions satisfactorily, and many disease germs and parasites have died off. Now is the time to select fishes if everything checks out well.

Unless you deal with a tropical fish store it is likely that you will only have a selection of the more common varieties of fishes from which to choose stock. Regardless of the source, though, attention should be paid to the environment in which the fishes are kept. The water should be clear, the tanks should not be overcrowded, and a shop that allows dead fishes to remain in the tanks should be shunned. The fishes should be swimming and not gasping for air at the surface or clustered around the aerator.

Examine fish carefully for blemishes, torn fins, and signs of disease. Avoid specimens atypical for their species.

Caution must be exercised when choosing fishes for a mixed aquarium as the larger fishes may harass and even eat the smaller ones. Check with the dealer to ensure that the fishes you select are compatible. If your dealer doesn't know which fishes are suitable to keep in a community tank, buy your fishes from someone who does know!

Introducing Fishes

Most fishes are transported in polyethylene bags. Care must be taken that the fishes are not exposed to extreme variations in temperature while in transit. Do not keep them inside the bags any longer than necessary. Keep the plastic bag insulated during transport.

Most aquarists float the bags on the surface of the wa-

FACING PAGE:
A lionhead goldfish is not an ordinary goldfish, it is
a fancy variety especially bred often for exhibition in
goldfish clubs abroad and in the United States.

Male guppies *(Poecilia reticulata)* are always more colorful than the females, which are larger and have less developed fins.

ter to equalize the temperature. It is also possible to equalize the temperatures by transferring the fish, together with the water, to a glass or metal container that will float on the surface of the water. Approximately 30 minutes later the waters are about the same temperature and the fish can be introduced into the tank. If the quality of the water supplied with the fish is not suspect, then the fish may be allowed to swim free by lowering the edge of the container and letting the waters mix. If there is any doubt about the water, however, it is best to net the fish and gently lower the net into the aquarium, allowing the fish to swim free. Never drop a fish onto the water surface.

Once a fish population has been established in a tank, realize that you take a risk every time you introduce a new fish. Additional fish are always suspect and should be quarantined for a week or so. The fish can be accommodated in an unfurnished tank where it can be closely observed for any indications of poor health. The same principle applies to plants. Every aquarium book offers this advice but hardly anyone takes it.

If you have only one tank any new fishes can be put in a large bowl or jar and floated in the tank. Be sure the fishes have enough room and air surface, and that they can't jump into the main tank. Only if you know for sure that the newly acquired fishes have been in a disease-free tank for at least a week can they be directly introduced into the main tank. Be sure to properly aerate your isolation tank, even if it floats in your regular tank.

An aquarium needs to be inspected daily to guarantee that all is well. An even closer watch should be kept on all the inhabitants for several weeks after the introduction of a new fish. Be prepared to render immediate treatment for any ailment that may occur. Become familiar with the normal state of affairs in the tank so that you can detect any signs of trouble at the earliest possible stages. Check the water, gravel, and plants in the tank, as well as the fishes. Take daily note of the temperature and register in your mind the smell of a healthy tank. Even slight deviations from the usual should be further examined. The first sign of trouble is abnormal behavior of the fish. You will have to consult a larger book for more information on fish behavior, but all you need to know now is that should the fishes' behavior change suddenly, suspect an aquarium problem . . . usually the water is too hot, too cold, deficient in oxygen or poisoned.

At breeding time the female zebra danio *(Brachydanio rerio)* is easy to recognize by her broad abdomen filled with eggs. Otherwise, the sexes look alike.

The food preferences of tropical fishes vary tremendously among different species. Some fishes are herbivorous, but the majority are omnivorous. This means that they consume both animal and vegetable matter although they tend to consume more vegetable than animal. The basic diet of many tropical fishes should therefore be predominantly vegetable food supplemented with animal food.

FOODS AND FEEDING

Better prepared foods have a high protein content and are fortified with vitamins and minerals. Many brands of these dried food contain a complete balanced diet for fishes. They are sold in various forms—flakes, pellets, granules, powders, and compressed tablets being the most common. All are designed especially for various types of fishes to keep them in prime condition. It is recommended to **vary foods as much as possible** in order to give the fishes an assortment. Such diversity aids in preventing dietary deficiency diseases in captive fishes. These "all purpose" foods may be supplemented with a little animal matter.

The value of live food is never to be underestimated. Live foods have a nutritional advantage over prepared foods as well as adding bulk and natural laxative to the diet. Tropical fishes have been known to live for years on a diet of dried food, but they cannot compare in respect to growth, finnage, and color with fishes whose diet has been supplemented with live food. It is well worth the extra trouble of obtaining various suitable invertebrates. Take care to ensure that no harmful organisms are introduced when feeding live foods. Some live foods such as daphnia, tubifex worms, and brine shrimp are usually available in petshops and the small quantities required may be obtained cheaply. Other popular animal foods include earth-

FACING PAGE;
Bottom photo: Brine shrimp eggs are collected from the natural habitat or culture ponds, dried, and packaged for retail and wholesale markets.

THE WORLD'S LARGEST SELECTION OF PET AND ANIMAL BOOKS

T.F.H. Publications publishes more than 900 books covering many hobby aspects (dogs,

. . CATS . . .

. . . BIRDS . .

. . . DOGS . .

. . . ANIMALS . . .

. . FISH . . .

cats, birds, fish, small animals, etc.), plus books dealing with more purely scientific aspects of the animal world (such as books about fossils, corals, sea shells, whales and octopuses). Whether you are a beginner or an advanced hobbyist you will find exactly what you're looking for among our complete listing of books. For a free catalog fill out the form on the other side of this page and mail it today. All T.F.H. books are recyclable.

Since 1952, *Tropical Fish Hobbyist* has been the source of accurate, up-to-the-minute, and fascinating information on every facet of the aquarium hobby. Join the more than 50,000 devoted readers worldwide who wouldn't miss a single issue.

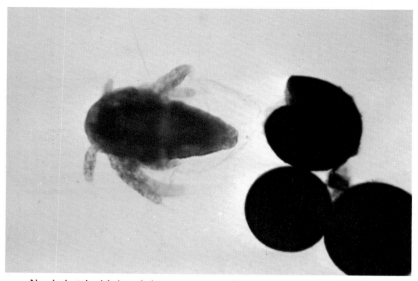

Newly hatched brine shrimp are among the most nutritious—and also among the most commonly available—foods for fish fry. Here (much enlarged) a brine shrimp nauplius is shown after having just left its egg.

worms, white worms, micro-worms, and infusoria. Live foods are often dispensed with because of the availability of frozen, freeze-dried, and canned foods, but no form of food is better than live food.

One of the most frequent causes of premature death among pet tropical fishes is incorrect feeding. The tendency of the beginner is to give too much at one time. Fishes eat far less than one expects, and any excess food not immediately consumed will sink to the bottom of the tank and eventually pollute the water. As a general rule, feed only as much at one time as the fishes can consume in 5 minutes. Also avoid excessively large or small particles. Try to give them pieces of food that can be easily found and comfortably swallowed.

As fishes are cold-blooded creatures, their metabolic rate decreases at low temperatures and they require little food. In fact, if the temperature is below 10°C (50°F) they will not feed at all. As the temperature of the water increases the fishes' appetite improves. At 24°C (75°F) they are good eaters and should be lightly fed twice daily.

The correct feeding of fishes is very important. When possible they should be fed at the same time every day, preferably once in the morning and once in the evening. The food

This guppy is very much interested in the bloodworms or larval chironomids (related to mosquitos) inside the feeding bell. However, these worms are too large to go through the holes of a device intended for much smaller live food, as brine shrimp or tubifex.

Flake foods are among the most popular of all dry foods. They are available in many different compositions and sizes and provide a very wide range of food choices for the fish. Photo courtesy Mardel Laboratories.

should always be placed in the same spot in the aquarium. The fishes will soon learn to anticipate feeding time. Check to see that the fishes are alert and eating normally each time you feed them.

If for any reason a meal is missed this will cause no harm to the fishes. Most fishes live quite happily for several days without being fed and during this time obtain some nourishment by nibbling at the water plants and the algae. You can leave on vacation for a few days and know that your fishes will survive rather nicely. Such a course is not recommended, though, and it is preferable to have a reliable friend regularly feed the fishes. If a non-fancier undertakes the task be sure to provide a few lessons in fishkeeping.

In the offices of T.F.H. Publications where exhibition tanks are maintained, the fishes are not fed on holidays and weekends, and they thrive for years.

Some varieties of tropical fishes are at their best in outdoor ponds. The advantages of keeping fishes in ponds are considerable: there are no aeration problems as the large surface area allows a substantial interchange of gases to take place; plants will grow freely; and there will be plenty of beneficial natural foods available for the fishes.

POND GARDENS

Primary consideration must be given to the placing of the pond. It should not be constructed near trees as falling autumn leaves will cause endless trouble. Leaves must be continually removed or they will sink, decompose, and upset the balance of a mature pond. The ideal site for a pond receives little sunlight on half its surface for most of the day. This ensures that the fishes always have access to shade and that the water does not overheat. Ponds for tropical aquarium fishes must never get lower than 50°F.

Commercially produced plastic ponds are rigid forms molded into the shape of the intended pond. They are typically of an informal design, have varying depths, and are the simplest of ponds to set. All that is required is excavation of a hole roughly the same size as the mold. Care should be taken to remove any sharp stones between the lining and the earth because the pressure of the water could damage the pond and cause leakage. When the mold has been set firmly into the ground by ramming earth down the sides into the empty spaces, the rim of the pond may be camouflaged with flat rocks. Plants may be added to give a more natural appearance.

Lined Ponds

This type of pond is slightly more difficult to construct but it is also the cheapest. All you need to purchase is a large

FACING PAGE;
An artificial pond can appear quite natural when properly prepared and planted.

sheet of thick gauge plastic. Dig out an area to the required shape and size. A minimum depth of 76 cm. (2½ ft.) is recommended at the center of the pool, gently sloping upwards to reach ground level at the edges. When the hole has been excavated the area should be raked carefully to smooth the contours and remove stones. The plastic sheeting is then laid in the hole with at least one foot of it bordering the edge of the pond. Heavy rocks are placed on this border to disguise the sheeting and also hold it in place. The excavated earth may be piled

A good liner is crucial in the construction of a garden pond. All the work is for naught if the ill-chosen liner breaks or rots within a short time. Plan ahead before embarking on this project.

around the rear and possibly one or two sides of the pond to make a rockery. The weight of the water will press the sheeting into the contours of the hole, providing an excellent lining. Plants must be set in containers around this sort of pond so that their roots do not penetrate the plastic sheeting. Many aquarium shops carry this type of garden pond material.

Pond Gardens

This kidney-shaped garden pond is decorated with natural stone on the exposed surface to reduce the stark appearance of bare concrete.

Concrete Ponds

This is usually the most expensive and the most difficult pond to construct. It is definitely the most permanent and reliable, though. With careful planning and a bit of effort, you can construct a landscaped pond which will provide an ideal home for fishes and will be an object of pleasure for many years to come.

The design of the pond may well depend on the existing layout of the garden. A plan of the pond should be drawn up and location, size, type of subsoil, and drainage considered before construction begins. Mark out the shape of the pond on

The plastic liner of this pond is completely hidden from view by a series of stone slabs. Adding a school of goldfish enhances its appearance further.

the site using pegs and string, remembering to allow for the thickness of the walls. The walls should slope slightly outward so that if the pond freezes over the ice will push upward instead of being forced squarely against the walls of the pond.

A drain is a valuable device when the time comes to empty the pond for cleaning. It should be at the deepest point in the pool and should direct the water into either a main drain or a dry well. A screwed-in vertical pipe is used to prevent overflow. A sink or bathtub plug makes a fine stopper and a piece of mesh positioned in the drain prevents debris from clogging the pipe. The dry well should be three times the volume of the pool and should be filled with large stones and rubble, allowing the entire contents of the pool to be drained at once. It would be satisfactory to have a small dry well and empty the bulk of the water first by siphon for general garden usage. When the pool is almost empty pull the plug and drain away the remainder. Of course all fishes must be removed prior to emptying the pool.

An overflow retains a constant level in the pool and prevents it from flooding out and washing in contaminants from the surrounding area. A vertical pipe connected to the drain works satisfactorily in maintaining the pond level. The pipe is screwed into a socket positioned in the drainage hole and then cut to the height of the desired water level. Any water above the top of the pipe will run into the drainage system and thereby maintain a constant level in the pond. Cover the end of the pipe with fine mesh to prevent unlucky fishes from being pulled into the pipe.

After the hole has been dug you can lay a lining of 100 gauge plastic sheeting or ram about three inches of rubble into the base. The excavated earth should be piled well away from the edge of the pond.

The cardinal rule to remember when laying concrete is that the pool should be laid in a single operation. Work from one end to the other, laying the base and sides as you go along.

FACING PAGE;
A waterfall can be created by the proper channeling
of the water into a receiving pool. Water is then
pumped back to the higher level once more.

Do not lay the base one day and the sides at a later date or the formed seams will be prone to leaks and encourage cracking if the pond freezes over. Shuttering for the sides of the pond should be made from wooden planks and situated so that the earth walls are the same distance from the shuttering all around the perimeter. An ideal concrete mixture is by volume one part cement, two parts sand, and three parts gravel or shingle. Mix the sand and cement together first using a hard, flat surface and then add the gravel. Water is mixed in slowly until the desired consistency is reached. Gradually adding the water ensures that it does not become too wet and runny to be easily managed.

The thickness of the concrete depends upon the size of the pond. A general rule is to make the base and sides of a 183 cm. (6 ft.) wide by 122 cm. (4 ft.) high by 76 cm. (2½ ft.) deep

Excessive growth of floating plants must be reduced, especially if fishes are present in a garden pool.

Waterlilies *(Nymphaea)* can grow very fast and completely cover a pond.

pond 10 cm. (4 in.) thick and increase the thickness by 1 cm. (½ in.) for every extra foot in length or width. Wire mesh may be set into the concrete for reinforcement, taking care that it does not poke through the surface. Concrete is placed between the shuttering and the earth wall, ensuring that every cavity is filled. Allow 72 hours for the concrete to set before removing the shuttering. Paint the inside with cement once the concrete has dried. If allowed to dry too quickly this finishing coat will not cure properly. Therefore, cover the surface with damp bur-

There are some wild aquatic flowering plants that can be cultivated in a garden pond or used to create a natural appearance along the edge of a pond.

lap and shade it from direct sunlight. Cover the pond with plastic if there is the likelihood of rain soon after the laying of the concrete. Fill the pond with water once the cement has dried and leave it for a week.

After the water has stood for a week drain it from the pond, scrub the concrete surface with a stiff brush, rinse it out, and let it dry. Apply a coat of surface sealer to make the pond completely leak-proof and also neutralize the effect of the lime in the cement which can be toxic to fishes and plants. Fill the pool again with water, leave it for 48 hours, drain, scrub, and rinse.

With a little ingenuity the pond can be made to blend in with its surroundings. A path of irregular paving can be laid around the edge of the pond and the excavated earth can be used for landscaping. A waterfall or fountain driven by a small electric pump increases the attractiveness of the pond and is also an asset to the health of the fishes.

In areas where winter is severe, draining and covering the pond from late fall to early spring is recommended. Water expands during freezing and causes the walls to crack.

Pond kits that contain both the water pumping equipment and the lighting equipment for the pond are available at pet shops. Photo courtesy of Rolf C. Hagen Corp.

Furnishing the Pond

The best time for planting is spring because the plants have time to establish themselves before winter sets in. Lay 5 cm. (2 in.) of clean, coarse sand in preparation. Many plants are suitable for pond living but most of them thrive at a depth of about 30 cm. (1 ft.) and so are best planted on shallow shelves. Plants may be purchased from local petshops with instructions on planting and care. No pond is really complete without a water lily or two. These are usually planted in submerged baskets near the center of the pond to add a touch of beauty as well as providing hiding places for the fishes. There are whole books written just about water lilies.

The pond may now be slowly filled with water. A heavy bucket placed on the bottom of the pool and water trickled into it avoids disturbing the sand base. Wait at least two weeks to allow the water to mature before introducing any fishes. Introduce a few less valuable fish to test the water.

Freshwater snails in the pond are beneficial as they act as scavengers and also help to control the growth of algae. If the pond is to be used for breeding, however, snails are best left out as they will consume large numbers of eggs. Frogs, as tadpoles, eat algae, too.

Maintenance of a well-balanced pond is a simple matter. Fallen leaves must regularly be removed from the water surface before they sink to the bottom. Every year it may be necessary to empty and clean a small pond. The best time of year to do this is late autumn after all the leaves have fallen. Plants should be thinned out, sludge removed, and the inside wall scrubbed down. Larger ponds need not be cleaned out every year but at least every other year is wise. During cleaning periods the fishes may be kept in well aerated tanks. Remember that when the water has been completely changed the fishes should not be returned to it immediately as the water once again needs to mature.

It is not necessary to change the sand at the bottom of the pond unless the water is polluted and the fishes are dying. The whole interior of the pond must then be disinfected with household bleach and thoroughly washed out so that no trace of the bleach remains.

Not long after constructing a garden pond an assortment of uninvited visitors appear. Many of these do not harm the fishes and some are even beneficial. Mosquito larvae, bloodworms, and caddisfly larvae are scavengers as well as valuable food for the fishes. If you really want a large, formal pool, have a contractor do it after you have read a few books on the subject.

FACING PAGE;
Ornaments for a garden pond can be both decorative and functional. The cornucopia of this statue hides the spout of water flowing into the pool. The flow of water can be stopped by a valve hidden from view. Many styles, sizes and shapes of such ornaments are available in garden supply stores.

A goldfish is an ideal garden pool fish. It can survive winter if the water is not too shallow and the deeper part of the pool remains unfrozen.

Selective breeding is preferred over random breeding by most aquarists. This means that tropical fishes of only one color variety are allowed to mate with each other. Therefore the young fish will be similar to their parents. To produce really good offspring the best parent fish are selected—

BREEDING

those showing the desirable characteristics of their variety. Although the sexes are separate in freshwater fishes as with most other vertebrates, it may be rather difficult to sex fishes outside the breeding season, except for livebearers.

Some species of fishes bear live young while others lay eggs. Since breeding techniques vary for different species of fishes the limited information presented in this book is offered merely as an overview. Consult other specialist books on breeding for details of particular species. Dr. Herbert R. Axelrod has written five books illustrated with wonderful photos, entitled *Breeding Aquarium Fishes*, Books 1-6. Look through them. They are quite informative.

Livebearers

Livebearers will often breed independently as long as they are well-fed and cared for. A lack of heat, light, or the presence of acid water can halt reproduction completely, though.

Males are typically smaller than females and usually have a gonopodium, an organ of copulation formed from a modified anal fin. A male will chase the female around the tank but she seems to take no notice. The male rushes in to eject his sperm at a given chance. The sperm can be stored in the female's reproductive tract for as long as six months, but most livebearers deliver every month.

FACING PAGE:
The guppy *(Poecilia reticulata)* is the most popular livebearer known to aquarists. Show guppies are often displayed in pet shops.

A pregnant mother swells unmistakably as the embryos develop. A yolk-sac nourishes the embryos while they lie within the female.

The main problem now is saving the young from being eaten by their parents and other fishes. Moving the female at this delicate stage, though, is likely to cause premature birth. She must be moved very early in her pregnancy so that the young are in no danger or very late so that they are so ready for birth that they will come to no harm when born.

To help save the young, many breeders arrange an assortment of plants to shelter the fry from their mother. The best plants, such as *Salvinia, Cabomba, Anacharis, Myriophyllum, Ambulia,* and *Nitella,* permit the young to dive to safety but are too dense for an adult to follow. The mother is removed at the earliest possible chance.

Liveborn fry are comparatively large. They can be offered prepared food, suitably small in size, at the outset. Feeding live food at this time is substantially beneficial to their growth rate. Microworms, newly hatched brine shrimp, and shedded tubifex are all recommended. The young should be fed several times a day and, unlike adults, they will not overeat. The temperature of the water should not be lower than 24°C. Fry thrive on high temperatures and full bellies.

Swordtails and platies tend to mate with their own kind but, given no other choice, some species will crossmate. Most of the hybrid offspring will be fertile.

Egglayers

The majority of aquarium fishes are egg scatterers. Most lay adhesive eggs which stick to plants. Some lay non-adhesive eggs which fall to the bottom of the tank. Most of the common egglayers are best bred in tanks with pebbles, glass marbles, or peat substituted for gravel, nylon mops replacing plants, and treated water (soft and acid). The peat traps any eggs, adhesive and non-adhesive, which drop to the tank bottom. As the spawning fish swim the peat is stirred up and covers the eggs so they remain uneaten. The pebbles and marbles do not permit the adults to feast on their eggs because the eggs

Breeding

Not all egglayers scatter eggs; some lay their eggs in a nest. This convict cichlid *(Cichlasoma nigrofasciatum)* is in the process of guarding the nest.

settle between them. Fishes that lay non-adhesive eggs should also be bred in shallow water of about 15 cm. The pair tends to spawn near the surface and shallow water means there is little time for the eggs to drop and the parents to intercept them.

The size of the tank is dependent on the fishes. Small fishes like white clouds or zebra danios of 5 cm. require 10-20 liter tanks, ½ cm. of peat, and one or two mops. Adjust the size and contents of the tank according to the size of the fishes. Always use the largest tank available. In addition, the tank should be well lit and have an adjustable temperature control. Most fishes spawn in water of 24°C (75°F), but a further rise in temperature may be required.

The majority of fishes have distinguishable sexes. Males are generally slimmer, smaller, and more brightly colored. At breeding time the female is bulging and full of spawn while the male is lively and well-colored.

When the pair is introduced into the tank, spawning may be immediate or it may take several days. In a few species

the female begins to chase the male, but ultimately it is the male who does the chasing. Spasms of egg laying accompanied by simultaneous fertilization may take an hour to a couple of days. Several hours is most typical.

It is best to watch the whole process so the parents can be removed before they eat the eggs. To prevent mating from occurring while you are not present, cover the tank to block out daylight or separate the pair with a glass divider. Nearly all fishes will eat the eggs if given the chance. It is unusual for the young of egg scatterers to survive in a community tank even if they are left with only their parents.

If the pair has not spawned in two days raise the temperature 2-3°C. If there has been no activity in two more days remove the fish and try again later.

Eggs are small and clear. Infertile eggs will become opaque and fungused. If peat is used, you may not be able to see the eggs easily.

The great majority of eggs hatch rapidly, usually in less than 24 hours. The young live on a yolk-sac for a few days. Most species then attach themselves to the glass, head upward and motionless, for another day or two until the yolk-sac is absorbed. Watch the yolk-sac go down for then it is time to feed the fry. For a time the young will remain close to the tank bottom in light and will swim freely in the darkness.

A festae cichlid (*Cichlasoma festae*) parent watching the fry. In contrast to egg scatterers, nest builders rarely devour their own spawn.

Newly hatched fry have prominent bellies and large eyes. The partially filled yolk sac, visible through the transparent skin, is gradually absorbed. If unable to feed, the fry will die of starvation.

Newly hatched fry are very delicate and should not be netted or moved. They could be killed by even a small drop in temperature, and dust on the water surface could prevent them from breaking the surface.

The young are very small and require special feeding. For the first few weeks they can feed only upon the most minute particles. It will be necessary to feed them small quantities of food several times a day as they will be quite ravenous.

The most common food for fry is suspended algae in the water. To obtain an algae suspension a glass container is filled with water and left outdoors. After about a week the water becomes green with suspended algae. To feed this to the fry remove a pint of water from the fry tank and replace it with the same quantity of the suspension.

Cultures of infusoria produced in jars are also excellent food for fry. Jars are filled with water to which a pinch of garden soil and a bruised lettuce leaf or a few strands of straw have been added. After a few days in a warm place the infusoria (a collection of semi-microscopic organisms) can be seen as a moving cloud in the jars. A few drops of culture added to the tank several times a day provide nutritious food for fry.

As the young reach four weeks of age they can begin to take larger food particles. Newly hatched brine shrimp makes the ideal food for fishes about a week old. Ask at your petshop for the eggs and details on hatching them.

HEALTH CARE

All living things are subject to disease, and fishes are no exception. Fishes generally have great resistance and when they succumb to parasites, fungi, or virus infections it is usually because they have been weakened by a poor environment. Unsuitable food, lack of oxygen, temperatures too high or too low, and other contributing factors are all the result of the keeper. Most ailments can therefore be avoided.

Symptoms to watch for in your tropical fishes include the following:

1. Loss of appetite
2. Sluggish and aimless swimming
3. Folded dorsal or caudal fin
4. Hanging from the surface or lying on the bottom
5. Slow reactions to disturbances
6. Rubbing against surfaces as if trying to scrape something off the body
7. Loss of luster
8. Ragged fins, lesions, white spots, or growths of any kind
9. Bloating or emaciation
10. Bulging eyes.

Should you notice your fishes exhibiting any of these symptoms consider carefully what might have triggered the problem:

1. Have any new fishes, plants, or water of doubtful purity been added to the aquarium, possibly introducing parasites or disease?

2. Has the tank environment deteriorated? Do the fishes have plenty of room and adequate aeration?

3. Have you been feeding inferior or improper foods or polluting the water by adding more food than the fishes can consume?

4. Have the fishes been receiving insufficient light or have they been "cooking" in a window?

Consideration of these points might give a clue as to what is wrong with the fishes. Often the trouble can be cured by remedying the flaw in the environment. Sometimes chemical treatment is necessary.

The aquarist is well advised to use drugs labelled for specific problems. Be wary of any substance that is claimed to be a cure for everything.

Medicines are usually administered by dissolving them in the water. If the substance is to be dissolved be sure that there are no particles remaining or these may be eaten by the fishes with disastrous results. Solutions can be filtered before adding them to the tank.

If individual fishes are suffering, isolate them immedi-

Sick fish may hide and remain unseen in a heavily planted tank, only to be discovered too late for treatment, like this African cichlid *(Haplochromis)* with tail rot and fungused body.

ately. If an entire tank or pond is affected then large scale measures must be taken. Consult a book on fish diseases or your local aquarium shop for help in identifying and treating fish diseases.

Hospital Tanks (Quarantine Tanks)

If individuals require treatment they must be isolated from the rest of the stock to prevent possible spread of the malady with a resulting epidemic. A small hospital or quarantine tank for this purpose should be unfurnished, have a stable temperature, and be situated in a quiet place away from bright lights. Sick fishes should have minimal disturbance to prevent them from becoming stressed. When you transfer the fishes to this tank include as much of its original water as possible to minimize the shock.

An isolation tank prevents a stick fish from infecting healthy fishes, the aquarium plants will not be damaged by chemicals, and more accurate doses of medication can be administered due to the small volume of water. Healthy fishes will not be able to harass weakened individuals, and once treatment is completed the tank can be easily sterilized. It also isolates the fish for easy, quick observation.

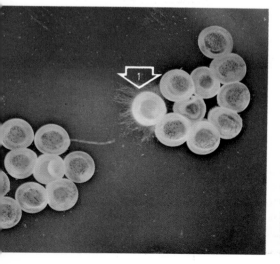

Fish eggs are most vulnerable to fungus, especially in poorly aerated water. The arrow points to one that is opaque, being already dead, with filaments of fungus growing on the surface.

Ponds

A fish that was not up to par in an aquarium would soon be noticed. In a pond where there are many fishes and many places for them to hide, it is not so easy to detect the symptoms until quite a few fishes have been affected. The pond keeper must be particularly vigilant, and if any fish comes to your attention as being slightly off color it should be dipped out and placed in a container for individual attention.

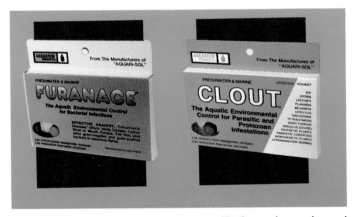

A number of medicines formulated to cure specific diseases in aquarium and pond fishes are available on the market; your pet dealer can recommend particular courses of treatment for commonly encountered diseases. Photo courtesy Aquarium Products.

Most problems are less likely to affect ponds than aquariums but are much more likely to be noticed in aquariums. Treatments for ponds and aquariums are basically the same, but of course the dosage of medication must be increased for ponds in proportion to the volume of water. Generally ponds are treated for the cause of the problem; fishes in the pond are not individually treated. Pond problems are usually water problems.

SALT-WATER AQUARIUMS

A salt-water or marine aquarium is more difficult to maintain than a freshwater tank, but with proper equipment and regular maintenance the incidence of problems is greatly reduced. Knowledge about the effects of salt water upon a tank and its occupants is vital for the successful operation of a marine tank. Marine fishes are considerably more expensive than freshwater species, but they are far and away the most exquisite and exotic specimens.

Much less dissolved oxygen is held in salt water than freshwater. Therefore, aeration is more critical to a marine tank for dispelling carbon dioxide and other harmful gases. A filter and adequate aeration are crucial to the success of a salt-water tank.

Salt water is more chemically active than freshwater. Care must be taken that no untreated metal contacts the salt water.

Freshwater plants cannot survive in salt water. Other furnishings, such as coral and shells, should be used to decorate the tank. Marine animals other than true fishes, like crabs, snails, and anemones, also add to the display.

Ideally, there is no substitute for filtered sea water. However, finding unpolluted sea water in most locales is certainly a feat. Several formulas for making artifical salt water are available on the market. These solutions should pose no problem to the fishes as those specimens you select in the pet shop have probably been in an artificial solution for some time.

The temperature is best kept between 78-80°F. Once a month 10% of the water is removed and replaced with a fresh solution. The salt concentration of the water in the tank needs to be kept constant so the concentration of the additional water is adjusted appropriately.

Feeding of marine fishes is the same as for freshwater,

however the salt-water species eat mostly frozen foods as opposed to flakes. Don't begin your aquarium experience with a salt-water tank. It is too expensive and too difficult. Start with a freshwater aquarium and after a year or more of success you can try your hand at a marine tank.

There are lots of books on salt-water aquarium fishes.

Be sure that the coral stone decoration to be used in a marine tank is completely clean. Once placed in water, coral polyps although dead and dried will rot and pollute the water.

The following books published by T.F.H. Publications are available at pet shops and book stores everywhere.

GENERAL AQUARIUM HANDBOOKS AND FISH CATALOGS

ALL ABOUT AQUARIUMS
Bu Earl Schneider
ISBN 0-87666-768-X
T.F.H. PS-601
   A very complete general introduction to the beginning aquarists or those just thinking about it. Excellent for pre-planning as you consider your options in setting up.

AQUARIUM KEEPING...
EASY AS ABC
By Werner Weiss
ISBN 0-87666-100-X
T.F.H. PS-831
   A beautiful large-format beginner's book that includes everything one needs to know to enter the "art" of fishkeeping—plenty about the tanks and the fishes too!

HANDBOOK OF TROPICAL AQUARIUM FISHES (New Edition)
By Drs. Herbert R. Axelrod and Leonard P. Schultz
ISBN 0-87666-491-5
PS-663 (Hardcover)
5½ x 8"; 736 pages
   Relied upon by many, many thousands of aquarists, this book is a classic. Covers everything.

STARTING YOUR TROPICAL AQUARIUM
By Dr. Herbert R. Axelrod
ISBN 0-86622-105-0
T.F.H. PS-840
   Contains a wealth of vlauable information not found in many other beginner's books, including a chapter on fish genetics and another on the naming of the cardinal tetra.

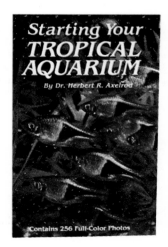

VIERKE'S AQUARIUM BOOK
By Jörg Vierke
ISBN 0-86622-103-4
T.F.H. PS-834

One of Germany's leading aquarists presents one of the most thorough aquarium books ever written, discussing virtually every aspect of aquarium keeping—much more than just fishes. Equipment, plants, breeding, feeding, and raising fishes are discussed in elaborate detail.

EXOTIC TROPICAL FISHES
EXPANDED EDITION
By Dr. Herbert R. Axelrod, Dr. C. W. Emmens, Dr. Warren E. Burgess, and Neal Pronek
ISBN 0-87666-543-1 (hardcover)
ISBN 0-87666-537-7 (looseleaf)
T.F.H. H-1028 (hardcover)
H-1028L (looseleaf)

The "bible" of freshwater ornamental fishes—contains comprehensive information on aquarium maintenance, plants, and commercial culture, as well as over 1,000 color photos and entries on many hundreds of species. New supplements are issued every month in *Tropical Fish Hobbyist* magazine, and may be placed into the looseleaf edition.

DISEASES OF AQUARIUM FISHES
By Dr. Robert J. Goldstein
ISBN 0-87666-795-7
T.F.H. PS-201

A discussion of many of the parasites most likely to be encountered by the aquarist, with suggestions on effective treatment.

DR. AXELROD'S ATLAS OF FRESHWATER AQUARIUM FISHES
By Dr. Herbert R. Axelrod, Dr. Warren E. Burgess, Neal Pronek, and Jerry G. Walls.
ISBN 0-86622-052-6
T.F.H.H-1077

The ultimate aquarium book—illustrated with over 4000 color photos. Almost every fish available to hobbyists is illustrated! Species are grouped geographically and by family for easy reference. No aquarist's library is complete without it!

DR. AXELROD'S MINI-ATLAS OF FRESHWATER AQUARIUM FISHES
By Dr. Herbert R. Axelrod, Dr. C. W. Emmens, Dr. Warren E. Burgess and others
ISBN 0-86622-385-1
H-1090

Smaller in size than the large Atlas on which it was patterned but still containing over 2000 full-color photos, this book contains even more general aquarium information about setting up and maintaining an aquarium, fish breeding, disease treatment, etc. Tremendous value.

AQUARIUM PLANTS
By Dr. Karel Rataj and T.J. Horeman
ISBN 0-87666-455-9
T.F.H. H-966

The most complete volume ever published about aquarium plants, it includes taxonomic information as well as ecology, reproduction and cultivation, and guides to proper aquarium lighting.

Index